# It's Time Again To Skip A Birthday When . . .

by
Cyrano De Words-u-lac

*It's Time Again*
*To Skip A Birthday When . . .*
ISBN 0-88144-180-5
Copyright © 1996 Dan and Dave Davidson
Rhymeo Ink
P.O. Box 1416
Salem, Virginia  24153

Application has been made for a registered federal trademark for "Rhymeo"
and "Show-It Poet."

Published by Trade Life Books
P.O. Box 55325
Tulsa, Oklahoma  74155

# WHAT'S A RHYMEO™?

Rhymeos™ are fat-free un-poetry — lite and lean literary cuisine. Rhymeos™ are short and sketchy, quick and catchy — two short lines reinforced in rhyme. Although the short rhyming couplets display a poetic flavor, they are not traditional poetry. They are actually jingles about life — Jingle Verse Poetry for the 21st Century — offering insight and motivation, humor and inspiration.

Cyrano De Words-u-lac pens the shortest verse in the universe — a story to tell in a nutshell, a rhyming report to make a long story short. Rhymeos™ are short and sweet and poetically petite — clever ways to paraphrase — bite-sized words to the wise. Whether concise advice or an easy doesy fuzzy wuzzy, Rhymeos™ give a reflective perspective in a fireside chat format. It's literary rap with a snap — poetically correct dialect — a way to cope with humor and hope!

## Clues To Let You Know
## When Candles Have To Go

If every year you find it becomes harder to handle
the thought of growing older and adding another candle,

Now Cyrano can help you carefully conclude
to know which birthday year to joyfully exclude.

If you know the secret of skipping your special day,
you're not over the hill, but on the mountain top to stay.

This list of Rhymeo™ clues can be a helpful gauge
to keep you feeling younger and to clip advancing age.

*Cyrano De Words-u-lac*

*dedication*

**to our father Don
and uncle Bill,
who both need to skip
a birthday**

# It's Time Again To Skip A Birthday When . . .

**It's Time Again To Skip A Birthday When...**

# your big adventure is cleaning a denture.

It's Time Again To Skip A Birthday When...

# your teeth sleep in a drink in a cup by the sink.

## It's Time Again To Skip A Birthday When...

### you feel dismal without Pepto Bismol®.

### you turn and churn with heartburn.

# you can't bend over to pet your dog Rover.

# the tummy sags and eyes have bags.

# you can pinch more than an inch.

**It's Time Again To Skip A Birthday When...**

# you can't rub-a-dub-dub anymore in the tub.

# life's long haul is hard to recall.

**you lose a twinkle
and gain a wrinkle.**

**you can't compete
with crow's feet.**

memory starts to
fade and you
stay in the shade.

# cake candles glow like a fireworks show.

# you're a field tester for polyester.

## It's Time Again To Skip A Birthday When...

kids are a tutor
for your computer.

you need a magnifier
to read the Sunday flyer.

20

# to walk uphill you need a pep pill.

## It's Time Again To Skip A Birthday When...

# one of your best friends is Depends®.

# you can't swing your pelvis anymore like Elvis.

It's Time Again To Skip A Birthday When...

# you give food extra spice and newlyweds advice.

# you have a devotion to soft skin lotion.

It's Time Again To Skip A Birthday When...

# skin is flaky
# and feet are shaky.

# it's hard to touch your toes or put on pantyhose.

# hips hobble
# and knees wobble.

28

# sitting in a chair
# you fall asleep or stare.

### world history isn't a mystery.

### you start off each page with "when I was your age . . ."

30

# A.A.R.P.
# is your cup of tea.

## It's Time Again To Skip A Birthday When...

**wear and tear
turns to Medicare.**

**your physique
feels antique.**

# you idolize those who exercise.

# the sun gets hot on your bald spot.

# you were alive before cars could drive.

## It's Time Again To Skip A Birthday When...

you try to forget
your birth certificate.

you can't handle
another candle.

# arthritis points to all your joints.

**It's Time Again To Skip A Birthday When...**

# muscles weaken
# and you start creakin'.

# you close the lid for a grandkid.

**It's Time Again To Skip A Birthday When...**

# your greatest ambition is the large print edition.

# your sacroiliac stays out of whack.

It's Time Again To Skip A Birthday When...

# it's no surprise
# you need the next size.

# you consider reduction with liposuction.

## It's Time Again To Skip A Birthday When...

**you huff and puff
getting off your duff.**

**your kids have grown
and you parent by phone.**

44

# you're compared to fine vintage wine.

# you're a shopper
# for a set of choppers.

# you often dream of wrinkle cream.

**It's Time Again To Skip A Birthday When...**

### you sulk and pout over hair falling out.

### you need to redesign a receding hairline.

48

## It's Time Again To Skip A Birthday When...

# at every hinge you feel a twinge.

**It's Time Again To Skip A Birthday When...**

## you can't prevent retirement.

## you're not a newlywed anymore in bed.

you play connect
the dots with
your age spots.

## It's Time Again To Skip A Birthday When...

**you're a might-have-been with a double chin.**

**you jump from juvenile to a senile lifestyle.**

every day you
compare new streaks
of gray hair.

## It's Time Again To Skip A Birthday When...

**you buy breath spray and extra Bengay®.**

# you lay on thick a lot of lipstick.

## It's Time Again To Skip A Birthday When...

**you feel like lead getting out of bed.**

**your only lingo is for weekly bingo.**

# the hokey-pokey isn't okey-dokey.

## It's Time Again To Skip A Birthday When...

**Boy Scouts compete
to help you cross the street.**

**your get-up-and-go
is simply too slow.**

58

to be a mover
and shaker you
need a pacemaker.

## It's Time Again To Skip A Birthday When...

you worry about slips
that could break hips.

all you're fit to do
is knit one purl two.

60

# youthful thunder has buckled under.

It's Time Again To Skip A Birthday When...

# it's hard to crunch raw veggies at lunch.

you have a neurosis
for osteoporosis.

## It's Time Again To Skip A Birthday When...

**anything new
is a big whoop-tee-do.**

**your taste buds
have become duds.**

your skin has blotches
and belts need notches.

## It's Time Again To Skip A Birthday When...

**you sing a song
and no one sings along.**

**your only fellowship
is on a senior bus trip.**

# you earn large amounts of senior discounts.

## It's Time Again To Skip A Birthday When...

**you snooze in the pews.**

**you have a spare rocking chair.**

# you find Metamucil®
## at times to be useful.

## you're a night time clapper light switch slapper.

you devote your soul
to the remote control.

## It's Time Again To Skip A Birthday When...

### it's customary
### to read each obituary.

### your cake torments
### fire departments.

# the doctor recommends no deep knee bends.

## It's Time Again To Skip A Birthday When...

nature calls on you
more than friends do.

you're visited a lot
to plan for a plot.

74

**you need an assistant with caps tamper resistant.**

## all you do
## is horseshoe.

## you think scoring
## is shuffle boarding.

## on windy days in May your toupee blows away.

**It's Time Again To Skip A Birthday When...**

# you have a variety of anxiety.

# you're abundant with the redundant.

## It's Time Again To Skip A Birthday When...

**you drive slow
with speeds below.**

**people mistake you
for a statue.**

**you yakkity-yak about a knick-knack.**

# old fashioned ways aren't just a phase.

# you've got the drive of an archive.

**It's Time Again To Skip A Birthday When...**

# you're a super-duper party pooper.

**It's Time Again To Skip A Birthday When...**

# you're quick to wrinkle like Rip Van Winkle.

# you're a moldy golden oldie.

you cut out cholesterol
and double up
on Geritol®.

## It's Time Again To Skip A Birthday When...

around the middle
you're not fit as a fiddle.

you add oat bran
to anything you can.

88

# you make a splash with a hot flash.

## It's Time Again To Skip A Birthday When...

**a pencil takes the place of eyebrows on your face.**

**you use Oil of Olay® twice everyday.**

# you survey skin for whiskers on your chin.

in the months of winter the south becomes your center.

you cash in your
annuity for a
retirement
community.

## It's Time Again To Skip A Birthday When...

you walk into a store and forget what you came for.

you've lost spark
in the dark.

# at the drop of a hat you adjust the thermostat.

## It's Time Again To Skip A Birthday When...

### your age group has flown the coop.

### the generation gap is your handicap.

# the stories you tell your friends know too well.

It's Time Again To Skip A Birthday When...

instead of him
or her, you're called
ma'am or sir.

## your hips can't swivel and skin starts to shrivel.

## you commit perjury about your plastic surgery.

## you have to squint to read fine print.

# it's a bear
# to walk up a stair.

## It's Time Again To Skip A Birthday When...

**others offer you their seat on a bus to rest your feet.**

**you cringe at the cause of menopause.**

# you look dynamite in dimmer light.

# your habitat
# is that of a pack rat.

# you wear wigs
# at shindigs.

# you fear the truth of the fountain of youth.

## It's Time Again To Skip A Birthday When...

**you become numb
from twiddling your thumb.**

**your heart's pitter pat
now flutters flat.**

# you need a prune by the afternoon.

# your potluck wish is a mushroom soup dish.

# you start to stoop and do the droop.

# It's Time Again To Skip A Birthday When...

# you're only a goer on a riding lawn mower.

# old Father Time says you're past your prime.

## you use Ex-lax®
## and facial mud packs.

## it seems your gums
## have the humdrums.

112

**you need to nap
after folding a map.**

**It's Time Again To Skip A Birthday When...**

# your happy returns resemble George Burns.

# you can't go low
# for the limbo.

## It's Time Again To Skip A Birthday When...

you fear the fate
of your prostate.

you always confide
in the TV Guide.

116

# you bring a lawn chair almost everywhere.

## It's Time Again To Skip A Birthday When...

**your ears hurt
after a concert.**

**your're a defender
of a suspender.**

# you admire the panel on the Weather Channel.

**It's Time Again To Skip A Birthday When...**

# you move like molasses with granny glasses.

# you look for elevators and escalators.

**robbing the cradle
could prove fatal.**

**follow through
is no can do.**

# you can't recall anything at all.

## It's Time Again To Skip A Birthday When...

**all your peers
are well beyond years.**

**you subscribe monthly
to Modern Maturity.**

# gone is your kick as a geriatric.

# it comes to historical view, no one can challenge you.

# Nick at Nite is your delight.

## It's Time Again To Skip A Birthday When...

**gravity starts
pulling your parts.**

**you need a girdle
and walk like a turtle.**

you search near
and far for your
parked car.

**your back gets the blues
just tying shoes.**

**you bequeath
false teeth.**

# you start fearing becoming hard of hearing.

## It's Time Again To Skip A Birthday When...

# it's revealed on a resume you weren't born yesterday.

# you're not a boaster of a roller coaster.

# the waitress thinks your plate has a senior discount rate.

## It's Time Again To Skip A Birthday When...

**you need a cane
to walk down memory lane.**

**you're taking the pay
from your I.R.A.**

almost everybody
thinks you're
a fuddy duddy.

# you admit boldly to "Sweatin' To The Oldies."

# you can't be cured from crossword.

# age clippers for birthday skippers

**It's Time Again To Skip A Birthday When...**

# save part of your wage for retirement age.

# fill out a will before you are ill.

# put some pep
# in your step.

have metabolism
optimism.

## It's Time Again To Skip A Birthday When...

# cut out caffeine from your routine.

# fill life with laughter happily ever after.

## It's Time Again To Skip A Birthday When...

**eat smart
for your heart.**

**make amends
with your friends.**

# always insist
# on being an optimist.

**It's Time Again To Skip A Birthday When...**

# care for your skin time and again.

# build self-esteem
# by doing your dream.

## It's Time Again To Skip A Birthday When...

**follow a plan
of fiber and bran.**

**be a witness
for health and fitness.**

# take time to floss to limit tooth loss.

## It's Time Again To Skip A Birthday When...

# don't let good taste go to your waist.

# have an annual medical physical.

## It's Time Again To Skip A Birthday When...

# take time to rest and feel your best.

# have a protocol to cut cholesterol.

## It's Time Again To Skip A Birthday When...

# take a vacation for relaxation.

# work to win
# the battle to be thin.

**prefer
adventure.**

**bolster bones
with hormones.**

# WHO IS CYRANO?

a literary
dignitary

a prolific writer
and poetic reciter

a word weaver
Rhymeo™ retriever

among supermen
of the fountain pen

## Cyrano De Words-u-lac
is the combined pen name of brothers
Dr. Dan the Man and Dave the Wave Davidson

## PARTNERS IN RHYME
the brothers behind Cyrano's mind
As legend has it, this modern day Show-It Poet™
is the great, great, grandson of the literary figure
Cyrano de Bergerac.

# A TALE TO KNOW BY CYRANO
## The Inspiration Behind A Legend In His Own Rhyme

Let me share with you a tale of inspiration and betrayal, a story of
poetic word, of my great, great granddad Cyrano de Bergerac.
For he had a tender heart and his nose was a work of art,
as a poet the part he played was that of a romantic serenade.
While another man spoke his prose, granddad hid behind his nose,
as the maiden was swayed by the rhyme of his friend's charade.
Generations later I found out about this hoax behind his snout,
and as a youth I felt betrayed by his phony masquerade.
I became ashamed of this mimicry and the heritage of my family,
but then one day I read by chance, the words he used for romance.
It was then when my heart realized the legacy of my family ties.
I saw him in a new light. My heart was touched, and now I write.
The prose composed from my pen, I propose as a new trend . . .
poetic proverbs known as Rhymeos™, by the Show-It Poet™ Cyrano,
Rearranged along this path of fame, was my granddad's last name,
no longer am I called de Bergerac; I am Cyrano De Words-u-lac.
If you find your lines are few, the words you lack I'll choose for you.
For I've pledged to become over time . . . a legend in my own rhyme.

# More Rhymeo™ Titles
## by Cyrano De Words-u-lac

Home and Heart Improvement For Men
A Mother's Love Is Made Up Of . . .
If I Could Live My Life Again . . .
Diamond Dreams

If you have a Rhymeo™ for Cyrano
send what you've penned to the
Quill Guild ™
for Rhymeo™ Writers, Readers & Friends of Cyrano

Write or call Cyrano to receive a FREE
Quill Guild™ Rhymeo™ newsletter or for information
on the **Life Story Inventory**™, **Grand Plow Plan** ™,
and **Diamond Dream** workshops;

Rhymeo Ink   P.O. Box 1416   Salem, VA 24153
CompuServe - 71175,1035   Prodigy - GCSU92A
America Online - rhymeo   E-mail - rhymeo@aol.com
phone (540) 989-0592   fax (540) 989-6176
1 8 0 0   4   R H Y M E O
visit the Rhymeo™ by Cyrano web site on the Internet
http://www.rhymeo.com